TWO FAT COWS

NIGEL TETLEY

Illustrated by Simon Goodway

Copyright © 2016 Nigel Tetley

All rights reserved. No part of this publication may be reproduced or transmitted in any form or by any means, electronic or mechanical including photocopying, recording or any information storage or retrieval system, without prior permission in writing from the publishers.

The right of Nigel Tetley to be identified as the author of this work has been asserted by him in accordance with the Copyright, Designs and Patents Act 1988.

Illustrated by Simon Goodway

First published in the United Kingdom in 2016 by The Choir Press

ISBN 978-1-910864-76-0

To Maggie Barwell

Acknowledgements

A modified version of the text of *Two Fat Cows* first appeared in *Eleven Dramatic Assemblies* (ZigZag Education, 2009), and is here reproduced by kind permission of the publisher.

Two fat cows
Called Marigold and Petal
Had eaten every blade of grass
And even every nettle.

Their field was bare and empty
And the day was getting late,
So, feeling rather hungry,
Petal strolled up to the gate.

"The field behind this gate
Is just the best I've ever seen,"
Said Petal as she stared
At all the grass so long and green.

Marigold said hopefully:
"Then open the gate! Be quick!
Undo the catch! Lean on the post!
And if that doesn't work, just kick!"

Petal tried her hardest,
But the gate was locked and sealed,
"I cannot move it," Petal said,
"We're trapped in this brown field."

"Not if I climb over it
And you crawl underneath,"
Said Marigold to Petal
As she smiled with gleaming teeth.

With that, the two fat cows
Began to carry out their plan,
And quickly made the strangest sight
Since time itself began.

With Petal squashed beneath the gate
And Marigold on top,
Both cows were stuck between two fields,
Their plan had failed full stop.

"This whole big mess is all your fault!"
Said Petal to her mate,
"I'm squashed beneath, you're straddled above
This horrid wooden gate!"

"Don't blame me!" said Marigold,
"My plan was fine and clever,
But we're just too round and fat
And now we're stuck like this for ever!"

And then the wooden gate
Began to creak and groan and bend
As Marigold's four legs hung over
Petal's, end to end.

Crash! Wallop! Thump!
The gate collapsed and Marigold dropped down,
The cows lay startled in between
Two fields: one green, one brown.

"We've done it!" shouted Petal,
"We've succeeded, me and you!
And not by going over, under,
Round or even through!"

"You're right, dear friend," said Marigold
Now climbing to her feet,
"No gate will ever stop us now,
The world is ours to eat!"

www.ingramcontent.com/pod-product-compliance
Lightning Source LLC
Chambersburg PA
CBHW041239020426
42331CB00002B/7